Sabor Natural

Receitas Veganas para um Estilo de Vida Sustentável

Ana Silva

Content

Roasted broccoli and beetroot 11

Roasted cauliflower and parsley 13

Roasted carrots and beets 15

Roasted cabbage and beets 17

Sichuan Style Roasted Broccoli 19

Roasted Cauliflower and Shitake Mushrooms 21

Spicy Roasted Carrots 23

Roasted smoked cauliflower 25

Baked enoki and pearl mushrooms 27

Roasted Spinach and Kale 29

Roasted watercress and broccoli 31

Roasted cabbage and kale 34

Three baked mushrooms 36

Roasted asparagus and beets 38

Roasted Cauliflower and Broccoli and Cabbage 40

Bean sprouts and roasted cauliflower 42

Roasted carrots and sweet potatoes 44

Roasted Purple Cabbage and Broccoli 46

Roasted Carrots with Butter and Mini Cabbage 49

Baked potatoes, carrots and Brussels sprouts 51

- Baked potatoes and asparagus 53
- Roasted French Asparagus and Sweet Potatoes 55
- Roasted parsnips and asparagus 57
- Carrots and asparagus with roasted garlic butter 59
- Roasted Asparagus with Garlic Lime Butter 61
- Roasted parsnips with lemon and garlic 63
- Roasted turnips and asparagus 66
- Roasted smoked parsley 68
- Roasted Broccoli and Asparagus 70
- Roasted Thai Cauliflower and Asparagus 72
- Asparagus and Lemon Baked Potatoes 74
- Roasted carrots and turnips with hazelnuts 76
- Roasted Italian Beetroot and Asparagus 78
- Yucca Root and Roasted Asparagus 80
- Roasted beets, turnips and asparagus 82
- Yucca root and roasted beets 84
- Potatoes with roasted hazelnuts and sweet potatoes 86
- Roasted Kohlrabi and Purple Yam 89
- Roasted Yams and Asparagus 91
- Roasted Asparagus and Parsley with Yucca Root 93
- Roasted Kohlrabi and Broccoli 95
- Roasted Broccoli and Carrots - Asian Style 97
- Brussel sprouts with balsamic glaze and roasted onions 99

Roasted purple cabbage and red onion 101

Mini Roasted Cabbage with Rainbow Peppercorns 105

Roasted Napa Cabbage with Balsamic Glaze 107

Roasted savoy cabbage and red onion 109

Roasted Red Cabbage with Balsamic Glaze............................... 111

Baked Shitake Mushrooms with Cherry Tomatoes 114

Roasted Parsnips and Button Mushrooms with Macadamia Nuts 116

Roasted button mushrooms with cherry tomatoes and pine nuts 118

Potatoes baked in the oven.. 120

Roasted spinach and parsley 122

Roasted Kale and Sweet Potatoes... 124

Sichuan-Style Roasted Watercress and Carrots...................... 126

Spicy and Spicy Roasted Turnips and Onions 128

carrots with carrots 131

Spicy Roasted Spinach and Onion 133

Sweet Potatoes and Roasted Spinach 135

Roasted turnips, onions and spinach 137

Watercress and carrots roasted in vegan butter 139

Roasted Broccoli and Spinach 141

Smoked roasted cauliflower and onions 143

Roasted Italian Beets and Kale.. 145

- Watercress and baked potatoes 149
- Roasted spinach with olives 151
- Roasted Spinach with Jalapeno Peppers 153
- Roasted Roasted Spinach 155
- Roasted Spicy Thai Bean Sprouts 157
- Szechuan Spinach and Spicy Turnips 159
- Carrots and onions with Thai watercress 161
- baked pastry and sweet potatoes 164
- White yam and baked potatoes 166
- Hungarian parsnips and turnips 168
- Plain Roasted Spinach 170
- Roasted Southeast Asian Spinach and Carrots 172
- Roasted Kale and Brussels Sprouts 174
- Spinach and baked potatoes 176
- Sweet potatoes with curry and kale 179
- Jalapeno Watercress and Parsnip 181
- Watercress and broccoli in chili garlic sauce 183
- Spicy Bok Choy and Broccoli 185
- Spinach and shiitake mushrooms 187
- Spinach and potatoes with pesto 189
- Roasted Sweet Potatoes and Kale 191
- Turnip greens and turnips with pesto sauce 193
- Swiss chard and carrots with pesto 195

Bok Choy and Carrots in a Chili Garlic Sauce 197

Slow Cooked Turnip Greens and Parsley 199

Slow Cooked Kale and Broccoli 200

Endive and carrots stewed in pesto 201

Braised Romaine Lettuce and Brussels Sprouts 203

Endive and boiled potatoes 204

Turnip greens and turnips slow cooked in vegan butter 206

Kale and Parsnip Slow Cooked in Vegan Butter 208

Chinese Style Spinach and Carrots 209

Bok Choy and Stewed Carrots 210

Micro greens and slow cooked potatoes 212

Kale leaves and slow cooked potatoes 214

Slow Cooker Cabbage and Potatoes 215

Boiled cabbage and carrots 217

Roasted broccoli and beetroot

Ingredients

1 ½ cups Brussels sprouts, chopped

1 cup large potato chunks

1 cup large carrot pieces

1 ½ cups broccoli florets

1 cup diced beets

1/2 cup yellow onion pieces

2 tablespoons of sesame oil

salt and ground black pepper to taste

Preheat your oven to 425 degrees F (220 degrees C).

Place the rack on the second lowest level of the oven.

Pour some salted water into a bowl.

Soak Brussels sprouts in salted water for 15 minutes and drain.

Put the rest of the ingredients together in a bowl.

Spread the vegetables in a single layer in a baking dish.

Bake until the vegetables begin to brown and cook, about 45 minutes.

Roasted cauliflower and parsley

Ingredients

1 ½ cups baby kale, chopped

1 cup large potato chunks

1 cup large parsley, diced

1 ½ cups cauliflower

1 cup diced beets

1/2 cup diced red onion

2 tablespoons of extra virgin olive oil

salt and ground black pepper to taste

Preheat your oven to 425 degrees F (220 degrees C).

Place the rack on the second lowest level of the oven.

Pour some salted water into a bowl.

Soak the mini-cabbage in salted water for 15 minutes and drain.

Put the rest of the ingredients together in a bowl.

Spread the vegetables in a single layer in a baking dish.

Bake until the vegetables begin to brown and cook, about 45 minutes.

Roasted carrots and beets

Ingredients

1 ½ cups purple cabbage, chopped

1 cup sweet potato chunks

1 cup large carrot pieces

1 ½ cups cauliflower

1 cup diced beets

1/2 cup diced red onion

2 tablespoons of extra virgin olive oil

salt and ground black pepper to taste

Preheat your oven to 425 degrees F (220 degrees C).

Place the rack on the second lowest level of the oven.

Pour some salted water into a bowl.

Soak the purple cabbage in salted water for 15 minutes and drain.

Put the rest of the ingredients together in a bowl.

Spread the vegetables in a single layer in a baking dish.

Bake until the vegetables begin to brown and cook, about 45 minutes.

Roasted cabbage and beets

Ingredients

½ cup Brussels sprouts, chopped

½ cup cabbage, chopped

½ cup purple cabbage

1 cup large potato chunks

1 cup large chunks of rainbow carrots

1 ½ cups cauliflower

1 cup diced beets

1/2 cup diced red onion

2 tablespoons of extra virgin olive oil

salt and ground black pepper to taste

Preheat your oven to 425 degrees F (220 degrees C).

Place the rack on the second lowest level of the oven.

Pour some salted water into a bowl.

Soak Brussels sprouts and sprouts in salted water for 15 minutes and drain.

Put the rest of the ingredients together in a bowl.

Spread the vegetables in a single layer in a baking dish.

Bake until the vegetables begin to brown and cook, about 45 minutes.

Sichuan Style Roasted Broccoli

Ingredients

1 ½ cups Brussels sprouts, chopped

1 cup broccoli florets

1 cup large chunks of rainbow carrots

1 ½ cups cauliflower

1 cup button mushrooms, sliced

1/2 cup diced red onion

2 tablespoons of sesame oil

½ tsp. Sichuan pepper

salt

ground black pepper to taste

Preheat your oven to 425 degrees F (220 degrees C).

Place the rack on the second lowest level of the oven.

Pour some salted water into a bowl.

Soak Brussels sprouts in salted water for 15 minutes and drain.

Put the rest of the ingredients together in a bowl.

Spread the vegetables in a single layer in a baking dish.

Bake until the vegetables begin to brown and cook, about 45 minutes.

Roasted Cauliflower and Shitake Mushrooms

Ingredients

1 ½ cups baby kale, chopped

1 cup shiitake mushrooms, sliced

1 cup large chunks of rainbow carrots

1 ½ cups cauliflower

1 cup button mushrooms, sliced

1/2 cup diced red onion

2 tablespoons of extra virgin olive oil

salt and ground black pepper to taste

Preheat your oven to 425 degrees F (220 degrees C).

Place the rack on the second lowest level of the oven.

Pour some salted water into a bowl.

Soak the mini-cabbage in salted water for 15 minutes and drain.

Put the rest of the ingredients together in a bowl.

Spread the vegetables in a single layer in a baking dish.

Bake until the vegetables begin to brown and cook, about 45 minutes.

Spicy Roasted Carrots

Ingredients

1 ½ cups Brussels sprouts, chopped

1 cup large potato chunks

1 cup large chunks of rainbow carrots

1 ½ cups cauliflower

1 cup diced beets

1/2 cup diced red onion

1 C. cumin

1 C. red pepper

2 tablespoons of extra virgin olive oil

salt and ground black pepper to taste

Preheat your oven to 425 degrees F (220 degrees C).

Place the rack on the second lowest level of the oven.

Pour some salted water into a bowl.

Soak Brussels sprouts in salted water for 15 minutes and drain.

Put the rest of the ingredients together in a bowl.

Spread the vegetables in a single layer in a baking dish.

Bake until the vegetables begin to brown and cook, about 45 minutes.

Roasted smoked cauliflower

Ingredients

1 ½ cups red cabbage, shredded

1 cup large potato chunks

1 cup large chunks of rainbow carrots

1 ½ cups cauliflower

1 cup diced beets

1/2 cup diced red onion

1 C. cumin

1 C. annatto seeds

1 C. paprika

1 C. chili powder

2 tablespoons of extra virgin olive oil

salt and ground black pepper to taste

Preheat your oven to 425 degrees F (220 degrees C).

Place the rack on the second lowest level of the oven.

Pour some salted water into a bowl.

Soak Brussels sprouts in salted water for 15 minutes and drain.

Put the rest of the ingredients together in a bowl.

Spread the vegetables in a single layer in a baking dish.

Bake until the vegetables begin to brown and cook, about 45 minutes.

Baked enoki and pearl mushrooms

Ingredients

1 ½ cups baby kale, chopped

1 cup broccoli florets

1 cup enoki mushrooms, sliced

1 ½ cups cauliflower

1 cup oyster mushrooms

1/2 cup diced red onion

2 tablespoons of canola oil

salt and ground black pepper to taste

Preheat your oven to 425 degrees F (220 degrees C).

Place the rack on the second lowest level of the oven.

Pour some salted water into a bowl.

Soak Brussels sprouts in salted water for 15 minutes and drain.

Put the rest of the ingredients together in a bowl.

Spread the vegetables in a single layer in a baking dish.

Bake until the vegetables begin to brown and cook, about 45 minutes.

Roasted Spinach and Kale

Ingredients

1 ½ cups Brussels sprouts, chopped

1 cup spinach, chopped

1 cup kale, coarsely chopped

1 ½ cups broccoli florets

1 cup cauliflower

1/2 cup diced red onion

2 tablespoons of extra virgin olive oil

Sea salt to taste

Ground black pepper to taste

Preheat your oven to 425 degrees F (220 degrees C).

Place the rack on the second lowest level of the oven.

Pour some salted water into a bowl.

Soak Brussels sprouts in salted water for 15 minutes and drain.

Put the rest of the ingredients together in a bowl.

Spread the vegetables in a single layer in a baking dish.

Bake until the vegetables begin to brown and cook, about 45 minutes.

Roasted watercress and broccoli

Ingredients

1 ½ cups Brussels sprouts, chopped

1 cup spinach, chopped

1 cup watercress, thinly sliced

1 ½ cups cauliflower

1 cup broccoli florets

1/2 cup diced red onion

2 tablespoons of extra virgin olive oil

Sea salt and ground rainbow pepper to taste

Preheat your oven to 425 degrees F (220 degrees C).

Place the rack on the second lowest level of the oven.

Pour some salted water into a bowl.

Soak Brussels sprouts in salted water for 15 minutes and drain.

Put the rest of the ingredients together in a bowl.

Spread the vegetables in a single layer in a baking dish.

Bake until the vegetables begin to brown and cook, about 45 minutes.

Roasted cabbage and kale

Ingredients

1 ½ cups baby kale, chopped

1 cup kale, coarsely chopped

1 cup large chunks of rainbow carrots

1 ½ cups cauliflower

1 cup button mushrooms, sliced

1/2 cup diced red onion

2 tablespoons melted vegan butter/margarine

salt and ground black pepper to taste

Preheat your oven to 425 degrees F (220 degrees C).

Place the rack on the second lowest level of the oven.

Pour some salted water into a bowl.

Soak Brussels sprouts in salted water for 15 minutes and drain.

Put the rest of the ingredients together in a bowl.

Spread the vegetables in a single layer in a baking dish.

Bake until the vegetables begin to brown and cook, about 45 minutes.

Three baked mushrooms

Ingredients

2 cups green beans, rinsed

1 cup oyster mushrooms

1 cup button mushrooms, sliced

1 ½ cups enoki mushrooms

1/2 cup diced red onion

2 tablespoons of extra virgin olive oil

salt and ground black pepper to taste

Preheat your oven to 425 degrees F (220 degrees C).

Place the rack on the second lowest level of the oven.

Pour some salted water into a bowl.

Soak the bean sprouts in salted water for 15 minutes and drain.

Put the rest of the ingredients together in a bowl.

Spread the vegetables in a single layer in a baking dish.

Bake until the vegetables begin to brown and cook, about 45 minutes.

Roasted asparagus and beets

Ingredients

1 ½ cups purple cabbage, chopped

1 cup bean sprouts

1 cup asparagus tips

1 ½ cups cauliflower

1 cup diced beets

1/2 cup diced red onion

2 tablespoons of sesame oil

Sea salt and ground black pepper to taste

Preheat your oven to 425 degrees F (220 degrees C).

Place the rack on the second lowest level of the oven.

Pour some salted water into a bowl.

Soak the purple cabbage in salted water for 15 minutes and drain.

Put the rest of the ingredients together in a bowl.

Spread the vegetables in a single layer in a baking dish.

Bake until the vegetables begin to brown and cook, about 45 minutes.

Roasted Cauliflower and Broccoli and Cabbage

Ingredients

1 ½ cups baby kale, chopped

1 cup bean sprouts

1 cup large chunks of rainbow carrots

1 ½ cups cauliflower

1 cup broccoli florets

1/2 cup diced red onion

2 tablespoons of canola oil

2 tablespoons. Thai Chili Garlic Paste

1 Thai basil

salt and ground black pepper to taste

Preheat your oven to 425 degrees F (220 degrees C).

Place the rack on the second lowest level of the oven.

Pour some salted water into a bowl.

Soak the mini-cabbage in salted water for 15 minutes and drain.

Put the rest of the ingredients together in a bowl.

Spread the vegetables in a single layer in a baking dish.

Bake until the vegetables begin to brown and cook, about 45 minutes.

Bean sprouts and roasted cauliflower

Ingredients

1 ½ cups green beans, chopped

1 cup large potato chunks

1 cup large carrot pieces

1 ½ cups cauliflower

1 cup diced beets

1/2 cup diced red onion

1 C. Spanish paprika

2 tablespoons of extra virgin olive oil

salt and ground black pepper to taste

Preheat your oven to 425 degrees F (220 degrees C).

Place the rack on the second lowest level of the oven.

Pour some salted water into a bowl.

Soak the bean sprouts in salted water for 15 minutes and drain.

Put the rest of the ingredients together in a bowl.

Spread the vegetables in a single layer in a baking dish.

Bake until the vegetables begin to brown and cook, about 45 minutes.

Roasted carrots and sweet potatoes

Ingredients

1 ½ cups baby kale, chopped

1 cup large potato chunks

1 cup large chunks of rainbow carrots

1 ½ cups sweet potato wedges

1 cup parsley

1/2 cup diced red onion

2 tablespoons of extra virgin olive oil

Sea salt

Rainbow pepper to taste

Preheat your oven to 425 degrees F (220 degrees C).

Place the rack on the second lowest level of the oven.

Pour some salted water into a bowl.

Soak the mini-cabbage in salted water for 15 minutes and drain.

Put the rest of the ingredients together in a bowl.

Spread the vegetables in a single layer in a baking dish.

Bake until the vegetables begin to brown and cook, about 45 minutes.

Roasted Purple Cabbage and Broccoli

Ingredients

1 ½ cups purple cabbage, chopped

1 cup large pieces of parsley

1 cup large chunks of rainbow carrots

1 ½ cups cauliflower

1 cup broccoli florets

1/2 cup diced red onion

2 tablespoons of canola oil

salt and ground black pepper to taste

Preheat your oven to 425 degrees F (220 degrees C).

Place the rack on the second lowest level of the oven.

Pour some salted water into a bowl.

Soak the purple cabbage in salted water for 15 minutes and drain.

Put the rest of the ingredients together in a bowl.

Spread the vegetables in a single layer in a baking dish.

Bake until the vegetables begin to brown and cook, about 45 minutes.

Roasted Carrots with Butter and Mini Cabbage

Ingredients

1 ½ cups baby kale, chopped

1 cup large potato chunks

1 cup large carrot pieces

1 ½ cups cauliflower

1 cup sweet potato chunks

1/2 cup diced red onion

2 tablespoons vegan butter/margarine

Sea salt and ground black pepper to taste

Preheat your oven to 425 degrees F (220 degrees C).

Place the rack on the second lowest level of the oven.

Pour some salted water into a bowl.

Soak the mini-cabbage in salted water for 15 minutes and drain.

Put the rest of the ingredients together in a bowl.

Spread the vegetables in a single layer in a baking dish.

Bake until the vegetables begin to brown and cook, about 45 minutes.

Baked potatoes, carrots and Brussels sprouts

Ingredients

1 ½ cups Brussels sprouts, chopped

1 cup large potato chunks

1 cup large chunks of rainbow carrots

1 ½ cups parsley

1 cup sweet potato

¼ cup minced garlic

2 tablespoons. lemon juice

2 tablespoons vegan butter/margarine

salt and ground black pepper to taste

Preheat your oven to 425 degrees F (220 degrees C).

Place the rack on the second lowest level of the oven.

Pour some salted water into a bowl.

Soak Brussels sprouts in salted water for 15 minutes and drain.

Put the rest of the ingredients together in a bowl.

Spread the vegetables in a single layer in a baking dish.

Bake until the vegetables begin to brown and cook, about 45 minutes.

Baked potatoes and asparagus

Ingredients

1 1/2 pounds potatoes, cut into chunks

2 tablespoons of extra virgin olive oil

12 cloves of garlic, thinly sliced

1 tablespoon. and 1 tbsp. dried rosemary

4 teaspoons of dried thyme

2 teaspoons of sea salt

1 bunch fresh asparagus, trimmed and cut into 1-inch pieces

Preheat your oven to 425 degrees F.

In a baking dish, combine the first 5 ingredients and 1/2 of the sea salt.

Cover with foil.

Bake for 20 minutes in the oven.

Mix the asparagus, oil and salt.

Cover and cook for about 15 minutes or until the potatoes are tender.

Increase your oven temperature to 450 degrees F.

Remove the nest and cook for 8 minutes, until the potatoes turn a light brown color.

Roasted French Asparagus and Sweet Potatoes

Ingredients

1 1/2 pounds sweet potatoes, cut into chunks

3 tablespoons of olive oil

12 cloves of garlic, thinly sliced

1 tablespoon. and 1 tbsp. dried rosemary

4 teaspoons of Provencal herbs

2 teaspoons of sea salt

1 bunch fresh asparagus, trimmed and cut into 1-inch pieces

Preheat your oven to 425 degrees F.

In a baking dish, combine the first 5 ingredients and 1/2 of the sea salt.

Cover with foil.

Bake for 20 minutes in the oven.

Mix the asparagus, oil and salt.

Cover and cook for about 15 minutes or until the sweet potatoes are tender.

Increase your oven temperature to 450 degrees F.

Remove the nest and cook for 8 minutes, until the potatoes turn a light brown color.

Roasted parsnips and asparagus

Ingredients

1 1/2 pounds parsley, chopped

2 tablespoons of extra virgin olive oil

12 cloves of garlic, thinly sliced

1 tablespoon. and 1 tbsp. Italian spices

4 teaspoons of dried thyme

2 teaspoons of sea salt

1 bunch fresh asparagus, trimmed and cut into 1-inch pieces

Preheat your oven to 425 degrees F.

In a baking dish, combine the first 5 ingredients and 1/2 of the sea salt.

Cover with foil.

Bake for 20 minutes in the oven.

Mix the asparagus, oil and salt.

Cover and cook for about 15 minutes, or until the parsley is tender.

Increase your oven temperature to 450 degrees F.

Remove the nest and cook for 8 minutes, until the potatoes turn a light brown color.

Carrots and asparagus with roasted garlic butter

Ingredients

1 1/2 pounds carrots, cut into chunks

4 tablespoons of melted vegan butter

12 cloves of garlic, thinly sliced

1 tablespoon. and 1 tbsp. dried rosemary

2 teaspoons of lemon juice

2 teaspoons of sea salt

1 bunch fresh asparagus, trimmed and cut into 1-inch pieces

Preheat your oven to 425 degrees F.

In a baking dish, combine the first 5 ingredients and 1/2 of the sea salt.

Cover with foil.

Bake for 20 minutes in the oven.

Mix the asparagus, oil and salt.

Cover and cook for about 15 minutes or until the potatoes are tender.

Increase your oven temperature to 450 degrees F.

Remove the nest and cook for 8 minutes, until the potatoes turn a light brown color.

Roasted Asparagus with Garlic Lime Butter

Ingredients

1 1/2 pounds potatoes, cut into chunks

4 tablespoons vegan butter/margarine

12 cloves of garlic, thinly sliced

2 tablespoons. lime juice

2 teaspoons of sea salt

1 bunch fresh asparagus, trimmed and cut into 1-inch pieces

Preheat your oven to 425 degrees F.

In a baking dish, combine the first 5 ingredients and 1/2 of the sea salt.

Cover with foil.

Bake for 20 minutes in the oven.

Mix the asparagus, oil and salt.

Cover and cook for about 15 minutes or until the potatoes are tender.

Increase your oven temperature to 450 degrees F.

Remove the nest and cook for 8 minutes, until the potatoes turn a light brown color.

Roasted parsnips with lemon and garlic

Ingredients

1 1/2 pounds parsley, chopped

6 tablespoons vegan butter/margarine

12 cloves of garlic, thinly sliced

2 tablespoons. lemon juice

4 teaspoons of dried thyme

2 teaspoons of sea salt

1 bunch fresh asparagus, trimmed and cut into 1-inch pieces

Preheat your oven to 425 degrees F.

In a baking dish, combine the first 5 ingredients and 1/2 of the sea salt.

Cover with foil.

Bake for 20 minutes in the oven.

Mix the asparagus, oil and salt.

Cover and cook for about 15 minutes, or until the parsley is tender.

Increase your oven temperature to 450 degrees F.

Remove the nest and cook for 8 minutes, until the potatoes turn a light brown color.

Roasted turnips and asparagus

Ingredients

1 1/2 pounds turnips, sliced

2 tablespoons of extra virgin olive oil

12 cloves of garlic, thinly sliced

1 tablespoon. dried rosemary

4 teaspoons of dried thyme

2 teaspoons of sea salt

1 bunch fresh asparagus, trimmed and cut into 1-inch pieces

Preheat your oven to 425 degrees F.

In a baking dish, combine the first 5 ingredients and 1/2 of the sea salt.

Cover with foil.

Bake for 20 minutes in the oven.

Mix the asparagus, oil and salt.

Cover and cook for about 15 minutes or until the turnips are tender.

Increase your oven temperature to 450 degrees F.

Remove the nest and cook for 8 minutes, until the potatoes turn a light brown color.

Roasted smoked parsley

Ingredients

1 1/2 pounds parsley, chopped

4 tablespoons extra virgin olive oil

12 cloves of garlic, thinly sliced

1 tablespoon. paprika

1 teaspoon cumin

2 teaspoons of sea salt

1 bunch fresh asparagus, trimmed and cut into 1-inch pieces

Preheat your oven to 425 degrees F.

In a baking dish, combine the first 5 ingredients and 1/2 of the sea salt.

Cover with foil.

Bake for 20 minutes in the oven.

Mix the asparagus, oil and salt.

Cover and cook for about 15 minutes, or until the parsley is tender.

Increase your oven temperature to 450 degrees F.

Remove the nest and cook for 8 minutes, until the potatoes turn a light brown color.

Roasted Broccoli and Asparagus

Ingredients

1 1/2 pounds broccoli, cut into pieces

3 tablespoons of extra virgin olive oil

12 cloves of garlic, thinly sliced

1 tablespoon. and 1 tbsp. dried rosemary

4 teaspoons of dried thyme

2 teaspoons of sea salt

1 bunch fresh asparagus, trimmed and cut into 1-inch pieces

Preheat your oven to 425 degrees F.

In a baking dish, combine the first 5 ingredients and 1/2 of the sea salt.

Cover with foil.

Bake for 20 minutes in the oven.

Mix the asparagus, oil and salt.

Cover and cook for about 15 minutes or until the broccoli is tender.

Increase your oven temperature to 450 degrees F.

Remove the nest and cook for 8 minutes, until the potatoes turn a light brown color.

Roasted Thai Cauliflower and Asparagus

Ingredients

1 1/2 pounds cauliflower, cut into pieces

2 tablespoons of sesame oil

10 cloves of garlic, thinly sliced

1 tablespoon. Thai Chili Garlic Paste

2 teaspoons chopped fresh Thai basil

2 teaspoons of sea salt

1 bunch fresh asparagus, trimmed and cut into 1-inch pieces

Preheat your oven to 425 degrees F.

In a baking dish, combine the first 5 ingredients and 1/2 of the sea salt.

Cover with foil.

Bake for 20 minutes in the oven.

Mix the asparagus, oil and salt.

Cover and cook for about 15 minutes or until the cauliflower is tender.

Increase your oven temperature to 450 degrees F.

Remove the nest and cook for 8 minutes, until the potatoes turn a light brown color.

Asparagus and Lemon Baked Potatoes

Ingredients

1 1/2 pounds potatoes, cut into chunks

2 tablespoons vegan butter or margarine

12 cloves of garlic, thinly sliced

1 tablespoon. lemon juice

1 C. annatto seeds

2 teaspoons of sea salt

1 bunch fresh asparagus, trimmed and cut into 1-inch pieces

Preheat your oven to 425 degrees F.

In a baking dish, combine the first 5 ingredients and 1/2 of the sea salt.

Cover with foil.

Bake for 20 minutes in the oven.

Mix the asparagus, oil and salt.

Cover and cook for about 15 minutes or until the potatoes are tender.

Increase your oven temperature to 450 degrees F.

Remove the nest and cook for 8 minutes, until the potatoes turn a light brown color.

Roasted carrots and turnips with hazelnuts

Ingredients

1/2 pound turnips, cut into chunks

½ pound carrots, cut into chunks

½ pound potatoes, cut into chunks

2 tablespoons of sesame oil

10 cloves of garlic, thinly sliced

1 C. 5 Chinese spice powder

2 teaspoons of sea salt

1 bunch fresh asparagus, trimmed and cut into 1-inch pieces

Preheat your oven to 425 degrees F.

In a baking dish, combine the first 6 ingredients and 1/2 of the sea salt.

Cover with foil.

Bake for 20 minutes in the oven.

Mix the asparagus, oil and salt.

Cover and cook for about 15 minutes or until the potatoes are tender.

Increase your oven temperature to 450 degrees F.

Remove the nest and cook for 8 minutes, until the potatoes turn a light brown color.

Roasted Italian Beetroot and Asparagus

Ingredients

1 1/2 pounds beets, cut into chunks

2 tablespoons of extra virgin olive oil

12 cloves of garlic, thinly sliced

1 C. Italian seasoning

4 teaspoons of dried thyme

2 teaspoons of sea salt

1 bunch fresh asparagus, trimmed and cut into 1-inch pieces

Preheat your oven to 425 degrees F.

In a baking dish, combine the first 5 ingredients and 1/2 of the sea salt.

Cover with foil.

Bake for 20 minutes in the oven.

Mix the asparagus, oil and salt.

Cover and cook for about 15 minutes or until the beets are tender.

Increase your oven temperature to 450 degrees F.

Remove the nest and cook for 8 minutes, until the potatoes turn a light brown color.

Yucca Root and Roasted Asparagus

Ingredients

½ pound yucca root, cut into pieces

1/2 pound potatoes, cut into chunks

2 tablespoons of extra virgin olive oil

12 cloves of garlic, thinly sliced

4 teaspoons of Provencal herbs

2 teaspoons of sea salt

1 bunch fresh asparagus, trimmed and cut into 1-inch pieces

Preheat your oven to 425 degrees F.

In a baking dish, combine the first 6 ingredients and 1/2 of the sea salt.

Cover with foil.

Bake for 20 minutes in the oven.

Mix the asparagus, oil and salt.

Cover and cook for about 15 minutes, or until the potatoes and yucca root are tender.

Increase your oven temperature to 450 degrees F.

Remove the nest and cook for 8 minutes, until the potatoes turn a light brown color.

Roasted beets, turnips and asparagus

Ingredients

1/2 pound carrots, cut into chunks

½ pound beets, cut into chunks

½ pound turnips, cut into chunks

2 tablespoons of extra virgin olive oil

12 cloves of garlic, thinly sliced

1 tablespoon. and 1 tbsp. dried rosemary

4 teaspoons of dried thyme

2 teaspoons of sea salt

1 bunch fresh asparagus, trimmed and cut into 1-inch pieces

Preheat your oven to 425 degrees F.

In a baking dish, combine the first 7 ingredients and 1/2 of the sea salt.

Cover with foil.

Bake for 20 minutes in the oven.

Mix the asparagus, oil and salt.

Cover and cook for about 15 minutes, or until the root vegetables are tender.

Increase your oven temperature to 450 degrees F.

Remove the nest and cook for 8 minutes, until the potatoes turn a light brown color.

Yucca root and roasted beets

Ingredients

1/2 pound chopped beets

½ pound yucca root, cut into pieces

½ pound turnips, cut into chunks

2 tablespoons of extra virgin olive oil

12 cloves of garlic, thinly sliced

1 tablespoon. and 1 tbsp. dried rosemary

4 teaspoons of dried thyme

2 teaspoons of sea salt

1 bunch fresh asparagus, trimmed and cut into 1-inch pieces

Preheat your oven to 425 degrees F.

In a baking dish, combine the first 7 ingredients and 1/2 of the sea salt.

Cover with foil.

Bake for 20 minutes in the oven.

Mix the asparagus, oil and salt.

Cover and cook for about 15 minutes, or until the root vegetables are tender.

Increase your oven temperature to 450 degrees F.

Remove the nest and cook for 8 minutes, until the potatoes turn a light brown color.

Potatoes with roasted hazelnuts and sweet potatoes

Ingredients

1/2 pound potatoes, cut into chunks

½ pound sweet potatoes, cut into chunks

2 tablespoons of macadamia nut oil

12 cloves of garlic, thinly sliced

1 tablespoon. and 1 tbsp. Herbs of Provence

2 teaspoons of sea salt

1 bunch fresh asparagus, trimmed and cut into 1-inch pieces

Preheat your oven to 425 degrees F.

In a baking dish, combine the first 6 ingredients and 1/2 of the sea salt.

Cover with foil.

Bake for 20 minutes in the oven.

Mix the asparagus, oil and salt.

Cover and cook for about 15 minutes, or until the root vegetables are tender.

Increase your oven temperature to 450 degrees F.

Remove the nest and cook for 8 minutes, until the potatoes turn a light brown color.

Roasted Kohlrabi and Purple Yam

Ingredients

1/2 pound potatoes, cut into chunks

½ pound kohlrabi, cut into pieces

½ pound sweet purple potato, cut into chunks

2 tablespoons of extra virgin olive oil

12 cloves of garlic, thinly sliced

1 tablespoon. and 1 tbsp. dried rosemary

4 teaspoons of dried thyme

2 teaspoons of sea salt

1 bunch fresh asparagus, trimmed and cut into 1-inch pieces

Preheat your oven to 425 degrees F.

In a baking dish, combine the first 7 ingredients and 1/2 of the sea salt.

Cover with foil.

Bake for 20 minutes in the oven.

Mix the asparagus, oil and salt.

Cover and cook for about 15 minutes, or until the root vegetables are tender.

Increase your oven temperature to 450 degrees F.

Remove the nest and cook for 8 minutes, until the potatoes turn a light brown color.

Roasted Yams and Asparagus

Ingredients

1/2 pound potatoes, cut into chunks

½ pound white pastry, cut into pieces

½ pound sweet potato

2 tablespoons canola olive oil

12 cloves of garlic, thinly sliced

2 tablespoons. Italian spices

2 teaspoons of sea salt

1 bunch fresh asparagus, trimmed and cut into 1-inch pieces

Preheat your oven to 425 degrees F.

In a baking dish, combine the first 6 ingredients and 1/2 of the sea salt.

Cover with foil.

Bake for 20 minutes in the oven.

Mix the asparagus, oil and salt.

Cover and cook for about 15 minutes, or until the root vegetables are tender.

Increase your oven temperature to 450 degrees F.

Remove the nest and cook for 8 minutes, until the potatoes turn a light brown color.

Roasted Asparagus and Parsley with Yucca Root

Ingredients

1 pound carrots, cut into chunks

½ pound parsley, chopped

½ pound yucca root

2 tablespoons of extra virgin olive oil

12 cloves of garlic, thinly sliced

1 tablespoon. and 1 tbsp. dried rosemary

4 teaspoons of dried thyme

2 teaspoons of sea salt

1 bunch fresh asparagus, trimmed and cut into 1-inch pieces

Preheat your oven to 425 degrees F.

In a baking dish, combine the first 7 ingredients and 1/2 of the sea salt.

Cover with foil.

Bake for 20 minutes in the oven.

Mix the asparagus, olive oil and salt.

Cover and cook for about 15 minutes, or until the root vegetables are tender.

Increase your oven temperature to 450 degrees F.

Remove the nest and cook for 8 minutes, until the potatoes turn a light brown color.

Roasted Kohlrabi and Broccoli

Ingredients

1/2 pound kohlrabi, cut into pieces

½ pound carrots, cut into chunks

½ pound of broccoli

2 tablespoons of extra virgin olive oil

12 cloves of garlic, thinly sliced

1 tablespoon. and 1 tbsp. dried rosemary

4 teaspoons of dried thyme

2 teaspoons of sea salt

1 bunch fresh asparagus, trimmed and cut into 1-inch pieces

Preheat your oven to 425 degrees F.

In a baking dish, combine the first 7 ingredients and 1/2 of the sea salt.

Cover with foil.

Bake for 20 minutes in the oven.

Mix the asparagus, olive oil and salt.

Cover and cook for about 15 minutes, or until the root vegetables are tender.

Increase your oven temperature to 450 degrees F.

Remove the nest and cook for 8 minutes, until the potatoes turn a light brown color.

Roasted Broccoli and Carrots - Asian Style

Ingredients

½ pound carrots, cut into chunks

½ pound broccoli, cut into pieces

½ pound cauliflower, cut into pieces

2 tablespoons of sesame oil

12 cloves of garlic, thinly sliced

1 tablespoon. and 1 tbsp. ginger, minced

4 teaspoons of onion

2 teaspoons of sea salt

1 bunch fresh asparagus, trimmed and cut into 1-inch pieces

Preheat your oven to 425 degrees F.

In a baking dish, combine the first 7 ingredients and 1/2 of the sea salt.

Cover with foil.

Bake for 20 minutes in the oven.

Mix the asparagus, olive oil and salt.

Cover and cook for about 15 minutes or until the potatoes are tender.

Increase your oven temperature to 450 degrees F.

Remove the nest and cook for 8 minutes, until the potatoes turn a light brown color.

Brussel sprouts with balsamic glaze and roasted onions

Ingredients

1 package (16 ounces) fresh Brussels sprouts

2 small red onions, thinly sliced

¼ cup and 1 tbsp. extra virgin olive oil, separated

1/4 teaspoon sea salt

1/4 teaspoon rainbow pepper

1 onion, chopped

1/4 cup balsamic vinegar

1 tablespoon fresh chopped rosemary

Preheat your oven to 425 degrees F (220 degrees C).

Butter a meal that is going into the oven.

Combine Brussels sprouts and onion in a bowl

Add 4 tablespoons of olive oil, salt and peppercorns

Toss to coat and spread the sprout mixture over the pan.

Roast until cabbage and onion are tender, about 25 to 30 minutes.

Heat the remaining tablespoon of olive oil in a small skillet over medium-high heat

Sauté the shallots until softened, about 5 minutes.

Add balsamic vinegar and cook until glaze reduces, about 5 minutes.

Add the rosemary to the balsamic glaze and pour over the cabbage.

Roasted purple cabbage and red onion

Ingredients

1 package (16 ounces) fresh purple cabbage, cut into quarters

2 small red onions, thinly sliced

¼ cup and 1 tbsp. extra virgin olive oil, separated

1/4 teaspoon sea salt

1/4 teaspoon ground black pepper

1 onion, chopped

1/4 cup red wine vinegar

1 tablespoon fresh chopped rosemary

Preheat your oven to 425 degrees F (220 degrees C).

Butter a meal that is going into the oven.

Mix the cabbage and onion in a bowl

Add 4 tablespoons of olive oil, salt and peppercorns

Toss to coat and spread the sprout mixture over the pan.

Roast until cabbage and onion are tender, about 25 to 30 minutes.

Heat the remaining tablespoon of olive oil in a small skillet over medium-high heat

Sauté the shallots until softened, about 5 minutes.

Add vinegar and cook until glaze reduces, about 5 minutes.

Add the rosemary to the balsamic glaze and pour over the cabbage.

Mini Roasted Cabbage with Rainbow Peppercorns

Ingredients

1 package (16 ounces) fresh baby kale

2 small red onions, thinly sliced

¼ cup and 1 tbsp. extra virgin olive oil, separated

1/4 teaspoon sea salt

1/4 teaspoon rainbow pepper

1 onion, chopped

1/4 cup balsamic vinegar

1 C. Herbs of Provence

Preheat your oven to 425 degrees F (220 degrees C).

Butter a meal that is going into the oven.

Mix the cabbage and onion in a bowl

Add 4 tablespoons of olive oil, salt and peppercorns

Toss to coat and spread the sprout mixture over the pan.

Roast until cabbage and onion are tender, about 25 to 30 minutes.

Heat the remaining tablespoon of olive oil in a small skillet over medium-high heat

Sauté the shallots until softened, about 5 minutes.

Add balsamic vinegar and cook until glaze reduces, about 5 minutes.

Add the Herbes de Provence to the balsamic glaze and pour over the cabbage.

Roasted Napa Cabbage with Balsamic Glaze

Ingredients

1 package (16 ounces) fresh Napa cabbage

2 small red onions, thinly sliced

¼ cup and 1 tbsp. extra virgin olive oil, separated

1/4 teaspoon sea salt

1/4 teaspoon rainbow pepper

1 onion, chopped

1/4 cup balsamic vinegar

1 C. Italian seasoning

Preheat your oven to 425 degrees F (220 degrees C).

Butter a meal that is going into the oven.

Mix the cabbage and onion in a bowl

Add 4 tablespoons of olive oil, salt and peppercorns

Toss to coat and spread the sprout mixture over the pan.

Roast until cabbage and onion are tender, about 25 to 30 minutes.

Heat the remaining tablespoon of olive oil in a small skillet over medium-high heat

Sauté the shallots until softened, about 5 minutes.

Add balsamic vinegar and cook until glaze reduces, about 5 minutes.

Add Italian seasoning to the balsamic glaze and pour over the cabbage.

Roasted savoy cabbage and red onion

Ingredients

1 package (16 ounces) fresh savoy cabbage

2 small red onions, thinly sliced

¼ cup and 1 tbsp. extra virgin olive oil, separated

1/4 teaspoon sea salt

1/4 teaspoon black peppercorns

1 onion, chopped

1/4 cup white wine vinegar

1 tablespoon fresh chopped rosemary

Preheat your oven to 425 degrees F (220 degrees C).

Butter a meal that is going into the oven.

Mix the cabbage and onion in a bowl

Add 4 tablespoons of olive oil, salt and peppercorns

Toss to coat and spread the sprout mixture over the pan.

Roast until cabbage and onion are tender, about 25 to 30 minutes.

Heat the remaining tablespoon of olive oil in a small skillet over medium-high heat

Sauté the shallots until softened, about 5 minutes.

Add the white wine vinegar and cook until the glaze is reduced, about 5 minutes.

Add the rosemary to the balsamic glaze and pour over the cabbage.

Roasted Red Cabbage with Balsamic Glaze

Ingredients

1 package (16 ounces) fresh red cabbage

2 small red onions, thinly sliced

¼ cup and 1 tbsp. extra virgin olive oil, separated

1/4 teaspoon sea salt

1/4 teaspoon rainbow pepper

1 onion, chopped

1/4 cup balsamic vinegar

1 tablespoon chopped fresh thyme

Preheat your oven to 425 degrees F (220 degrees C).

Butter a meal that is going into the oven.

Mix the cabbage and onion in a bowl

Add 4 tablespoons of olive oil, salt and peppercorns

Toss to coat and spread the sprout mixture over the pan.

Roast until cabbage and onion are tender, about 25 to 30 minutes.

Heat the remaining tablespoon of olive oil in a small skillet over medium-high heat

Sauté the shallots until softened, about 5 minutes.

Add balsamic vinegar and cook until glaze reduces, about 5 minutes.

Add the thyme to the balsamic glaze and pour over the cabbage.

Baked Shitake Mushrooms with Cherry Tomatoes

Ingredients

1 kilo of turnips, halved

2 tablespoons of extra virgin olive oil

1/2 pound shiitake mushrooms

8 unpeeled garlic cloves

3 spoons of sesame oil

sea salt and ground black pepper to taste

1/4 pound cherry tomatoes

3 tablespoons of roasted cashews

1/4 pound spinach, thinly sliced

Preheat your oven to 425 degrees F.

Spread the potatoes in a pan

Brush them with 2 spoons of oil and bake them for 15 minutes, turning once.

Add the mushrooms stem side up

Add the garlic cloves to the pan and cook until lightly browned

Drizzle with 1 tablespoon sesame oil and season with sea salt and black pepper.

Return to the oven and cook for 5 minutes.

Add the cherry tomatoes to the pan.

Return to oven and cook until mushrooms are tender, 5 min.

Sprinkle cashews over potatoes and mushrooms.

Serve with spinach.

Roasted Parsnips and Button Mushrooms with Macadamia Nuts

Ingredients

1 pound parsley, halved

2 tablespoons of extra virgin olive oil

1/2 pound button mushrooms

8 unpeeled garlic cloves

2 tablespoons chopped fresh thyme

1 tablespoon extra virgin olive oil

sea salt and ground black pepper to taste

1/4 pound cherry tomatoes

3 tablespoons roasted macadamia nuts

1/4 pound spinach, thinly sliced

Preheat your oven to 425 degrees F.

Spread the parsley in a pan

Brush them with 2 spoons of olive oil and bake them for 15 minutes, turning once.

Add the mushrooms stem side up

Add the garlic cloves to the pan and cook until lightly browned

Sprinkle with thyme.

Drizzle with 1 tablespoon olive oil and season with sea salt and black pepper.

Return to the oven and cook for 5 minutes.

Add the cherry tomatoes to the pan.

Return to oven and cook until mushrooms are tender, 5 min.

Sprinkle the macadamia nuts over the potatoes and mushrooms.

Serve with spinach.

Roasted button mushrooms with cherry tomatoes and pine nuts

Ingredients

1 pound of potatoes, halved

2 tablespoons of extra virgin olive oil

1/2 pound button mushrooms

8 unpeeled garlic cloves

2 tablespoons. cumin

1 C. annatto seed

½ tsp. Red pepper

1 tablespoon extra virgin olive oil

sea salt and ground black pepper to taste

1/4 pound cherry tomatoes

3 tablespoons toasted pine nuts

1/4 pound spinach, thinly sliced

Preheat your oven to 425 degrees F.

Spread the potatoes in a pan

Brush them with 2 spoons of olive oil and bake them for 15 minutes, turning once.

Add the mushrooms stem side up

Add the garlic cloves to the pan and cook until lightly browned

Sprinkle with cumin, red pepper and annatto seeds.

Drizzle with 1 tablespoon olive oil and season with sea salt and black pepper.

Return to the oven and cook for 5 minutes.

Add the cherry tomatoes to the pan.

Return to oven and cook until mushrooms are tender, 5 min.

Sprinkle pine nuts over potatoes and mushrooms.

Serve with spinach.

Potatoes baked in the oven

INGREDIENTS

1 ½ pounds potatoes, peeled and cut into 1-inch pieces

½ onion, thinly sliced

cup of water

½ vegetable stock cube, crushed

1 tablespoon. extra virgin olive oil

½ teaspoon cumin

½ teaspoon ground coriander

½ teaspoon garam masala

½ teaspoon chili powder

Black pepper

½ pound fresh spinach, coarsely chopped

Put all the ingredients in a slow cooker, except the last one.

Top with handfuls of spinach and fill the slow cooker with it.

If you can't get them all together, let the first batch cook first and add a little more spinach.

Cook for 3 or 4 hours on medium heat until the potatoes are tender.

Scrape the sides and serve.

Roasted spinach and parsley

INGREDIENTS

1 ½ pounds parsley, peeled and cut into 1-inch pieces

½ red onion, thinly sliced

cup of water

½ vegetable stock cube, crushed

1 tablespoon. extra virgin olive oil

½ teaspoon cumin

½ teaspoon annatto seeds

½ teaspoon cayenne pepper

½ teaspoon chili powder

Black pepper

½ pound fresh spinach, coarsely chopped

Put all the ingredients in a slow cooker, except the last one.

Top with handfuls of spinach and fill the slow cooker with it.

If you can't get them all together, let the first batch cook first and add a little more spinach.

Cook for 3 or 4 hours on medium heat until the potatoes are tender.

Scrape the sides and serve.

Roasted Kale and Sweet Potatoes

INGREDIENTS

1 ½ pounds sweet potatoes, peeled and cut into 1-inch pieces

½ onion, thinly sliced

cup of water

½ vegetable stock cube, crushed

1 tablespoon. extra virgin olive oil

½ teaspoon cumin

½ teaspoon jalapeno peppers, minced

½ teaspoon paprika

½ teaspoon chili powder

Black pepper

½ pound fresh kale, thinly sliced

Put all the ingredients in a slow cooker, except the last one.

Top with handfuls of kale and fill the slow cooker with it.

If you can't get them all together, let the first batch cook first and add a little more kale.

Cook for 3 or 4 hours on medium heat until the potatoes are tender.

Scrape the sides and serve.

Sichuan-Style Roasted Watercress and Carrots

INGREDIENTS

1 ½ pounds carrots, peeled and cut into 1-inch pieces

½ red onion, thinly sliced

cup of water

½ vegetable stock cube, crushed

1 tablespoon. sesame oil

½ teaspoon Chinese 5-spice powder

½ teaspoon Sichuan pepper

½ teaspoon chili powder

Black pepper

½ pound fresh watercress, thinly sliced

Put all the ingredients in a slow cooker, except the last one.

Garnish with a few handfuls of watercress and fill the slow cooker with it.

If you can't get them all together, let the first batch cook first and add a little more watercress.

Cook for 3 or 4 hours over medium heat until the carrots are tender.

Scrape the sides and serve.

Spicy and Spicy Roasted Turnips and Onions

INGREDIENTS

1 ½ pounds turnips, peeled and cut into 1-inch pieces

½ onion, thinly sliced

cup of water

½ vegetable stock cube, crushed

1 tablespoon. extra virgin olive oil

½ teaspoon cumin

½ teaspoon annatto seeds

½ teaspoon cayenne pepper

½ teaspoon lemon juice

Black pepper

½ pound fresh spinach, coarsely chopped

Put all the ingredients in a slow cooker, except the last one.

Top with handfuls of spinach and fill the slow cooker with it.

If you can't get them all together, let the first batch cook first and add a little more spinach.

Cook for 3 or 4 hours over medium heat until the root vegetables are tender.

Scrape the sides and serve.

carrots with carrots

INGREDIENTS

1 ½ pounds carrots, peeled and cut into 1-inch pieces

½ onion, thinly sliced

cup of water

½ vegetable stock cube, crushed

1 tablespoon. extra virgin olive oil

½ teaspoon cumin

½ teaspoon ground coriander

½ teaspoon garam masala

½ teaspoon chili powder

Black pepper

½ pound fresh kale, thinly sliced

Put all the ingredients in a slow cooker, except the last one.

Top with handfuls of kale and fill the slow cooker with it.

If you can't get them all together, let the first batch cook first and add a little more kale.

Cook for 3 or 4 hours over medium heat until the root vegetables are tender.

Scrape the sides and serve.

Spicy Roasted Spinach and Onion

INGREDIENTS

1 ½ pounds carrots, peeled and cut into 1-inch pieces

½ onion, thinly sliced

cup of water

½ vegetable stock cube, crushed

1 tablespoon. extra virgin olive oil

½ teaspoon cumin

½ teaspoon annatto seeds

½ teaspoon cayenne pepper

½ teaspoon lemon juice

Black pepper

½ pound fresh spinach, coarsely chopped

Put all the ingredients in a slow cooker, except the last one.

Top with handfuls of spinach and fill the slow cooker with it.

If you can't get them all together, let the first batch cook first and add a little more spinach.

Cook for 3 or 4 hours over medium heat until the root vegetables are tender.

Scrape the sides and serve.

Sweet Potatoes and Roasted Spinach

INGREDIENTS

1 ½ pounds sweet potatoes, peeled and cut into 1-inch pieces

½ onion, thinly sliced

cup of water

½ vegetable stock cube, crushed

2 tablespoons. vegan butter or margarine

½ teaspoon Herbes de Provence

½ teaspoon thyme

½ teaspoon chili powder

Black pepper

½ pound fresh spinach, coarsely chopped

Put all the ingredients in a slow cooker, except the last one.

Top with handfuls of spinach and fill the slow cooker with it.

If you can't get them all together, let the first batch cook first and add a little more spinach.

Cook for 3 or 4 hours on medium heat until the potatoes are tender.

Scrape the sides and serve.

Roasted turnips, onions and spinach

INGREDIENTS

1 ½ pounds turnips, peeled and cut into 1-inch pieces

½ onion, thinly sliced

cup of water

½ vegetable stock cube, crushed

1 tablespoon. extra virgin olive oil

2 tablespoons. minced garlic

½ teaspoon lemon juice

½ teaspoon chili powder

Black pepper

½ pound fresh spinach, coarsely chopped

Put all the ingredients in a slow cooker, except the last one.

Top with handfuls of spinach and fill the slow cooker with it.

If you can't get them all together, let the first batch cook first and add a little more spinach.

Cook for 3 or 4 hours on medium heat until the turnips are soft.

Scrape the sides and serve.

Watercress and carrots roasted in vegan butter

INGREDIENTS

1 ½ pounds carrots, peeled and cut into 1-inch pieces

½ onion, thinly sliced

cup of water

½ vegetable stock cube, crushed

1 tablespoon. vegan butter/margarine

1 teaspoon garlic, minced

½ teaspoon lemon juice

Black pepper

½ pound fresh watercress, thinly sliced

Put all the ingredients in a slow cooker, except the last one.

Garnish with a few handfuls of watercress and fill the slow cooker with it.

If you can't get them all together, let the first batch cook first and add a little more watercress.

Cook for 3 or 4 hours over medium heat until the carrots are tender.

Scrape the sides and serve.

Roasted Broccoli and Spinach

INGREDIENTS

1 ½ pounds broccoli florets

½ onion, thinly sliced

cup of water

½ vegetable stock cube, crushed

1 tablespoon. extra virgin olive oil

½ teaspoon cumin

½ teaspoon chili powder

Black pepper

½ pound fresh spinach, coarsely chopped

Put all the ingredients in a slow cooker, except the last one.

Top with handfuls of spinach and fill the slow cooker with it.

If you can't get them all together, let the first batch cook first and add a little more spinach.

Cook for 3 or 4 hours over medium heat until the broccoli is tender.

Scrape the sides and serve.

Smoked roasted cauliflower and onions

INGREDIENTS

1 ½ pounds cauliflower, peeled and cut into 1-inch pieces

½ red onion, thinly sliced

cup of water

½ vegetable stock cube, crushed

1 tablespoon. extra virgin olive oil

½ teaspoon cumin

½ teaspoon chili powder

Black pepper

½ pound fresh spinach, coarsely chopped

Put all the ingredients in a slow cooker, except the last one.

Top with handfuls of spinach and fill the slow cooker with it.

If you can't get them all together, let the first batch cook first and add a little more spinach.

Cook for 3 or 4 hours on medium heat until the potatoes are tender.

Scrape the sides and serve.

Roasted Italian Beets and Kale

INGREDIENTS

1 ½ pounds beets, peeled and cut into 1-inch pieces

½ red onion, thinly sliced

cup of water

½ vegetable stock cube, crushed

1 tablespoon. extra virgin olive oil

½ teaspoon Italian seasoning

Black pepper

½ pound fresh kale, thinly sliced

Put all the ingredients in a slow cooker, except the last one.

Top with handfuls of kale and fill the slow cooker with it.

If you can't get them all together, let the first batch cook first and add a little more kale.

Cook for 3 or 4 hours over medium heat until the beets are tender.

Scrape the sides and serve.

Watercress and baked potatoes

INGREDIENTS

1 ½ pounds potatoes, peeled and cut into 1-inch pieces

½ onion, thinly sliced

cup of water

½ vegetable stock cube, crushed

1 tablespoon. olive oil

½ teaspoon grated ginger

2 lemon branches

½ teaspoon green onions, chopped

½ teaspoon chili powder

Black pepper

½ pound watercress, thinly sliced

Put all the ingredients in a slow cooker, except the last one.

Garnish with a few handfuls of watercress and fill the slow cooker with it.

If you can't get them all together, let the first batch cook first and add a little more watercress.

Cook for 3 or 4 hours on medium heat until the potatoes are tender.

Scrape the sides and serve.

Roasted spinach with olives

INGREDIENTS

1 ½ pounds potatoes, peeled and cut into 1-inch pieces

½ green olives, thinly sliced

cup of water

½ vegetable stock cube, crushed

1 tablespoon. extra virgin olive oil

½ teaspoon cumin

½ teaspoon chili powder

Black pepper

½ pound fresh spinach, coarsely chopped

Put all the ingredients in a slow cooker, except the last one.

Top with handfuls of spinach and fill the slow cooker with it.

If you can't get them all together, let the first batch cook first and add a little more spinach.

Cook for 3 or 4 hours on medium heat until the potatoes are tender.

Scrape the sides and serve.

Roasted Spinach with Jalapeno Peppers

INGREDIENTS

1 ½ pounds broccoli florets

½ onion, thinly sliced

cup of water

½ vegetable stock cube, crushed

1 tablespoon. extra virgin olive oil

½ teaspoon cumin

8 jalapeno peppers, finely chopped

1 ancho pepper

½ teaspoon chili powder

Black pepper

½ pound fresh spinach, coarsely chopped

Put all the ingredients in a slow cooker, except the last one.

Top with handfuls of spinach and fill the slow cooker with it.

If you can't get them all together, let the first batch cook first and add a little more spinach.

Cook for 3 or 4 hours over medium heat until the broccoli is tender.

Scrape the sides and serve.

Roasted Roasted Spinach

INGREDIENTS

1 ½ pounds potatoes, peeled and cut into 1-inch pieces

½ onion, thinly sliced

cup of water

½ vegetable stock cube, crushed

1 tablespoon. extra virgin olive oil

½ teaspoon cumin

½ teaspoon ground coriander

½ teaspoon garam masala

½ teaspoon chili powder

Black pepper

½ pound fresh spinach, coarsely chopped

Put all the ingredients in a slow cooker, except the last one.

Top with handfuls of spinach and fill the slow cooker with it.

If you can't get them all together, let the first batch cook first and add a little more spinach.

Cook for 3 or 4 hours on medium heat until the potatoes are tender.

Scrape the sides and serve.

Roasted Spicy Thai Bean Sprouts

INGREDIENTS

1 ½ pounds cauliflower, blanched (soaked in boiling water and then iced)

½ cup green beans, rinsed

½ cup of water

½ vegetable stock cube, crushed

1 tablespoon. sesame oil

½ teaspoon Thai chili paste

½ teaspoon Sriracha hot sauce

½ teaspoon chili powder

2 Thai bird's eye chilies, minced

Black pepper

½ pound fresh spinach, coarsely chopped

Put all the ingredients in a slow cooker, except the last one.

Top with handfuls of spinach and fill the slow cooker with it.

If you can't get them all together, let the first batch cook first and add a little more spinach.

Cook for 3 or 4 hours on medium heat until the potatoes are tender.

Scrape the sides and serve.

Szechuan Spinach and Spicy Turnips

INGREDIENTS

1 ½ pounds turnips, peeled and cut into 1-inch pieces

½ onion, thinly sliced

cup of water

½ vegetable stock cube, crushed

1 tablespoon. sesame oil

½ teaspoon of chili paste

½ teaspoon Sichuan pepper

1 star anise

2 Thai bird's eye chilies, minced

Black pepper

½ pound fresh spinach, coarsely chopped

Put all the ingredients in a slow cooker, except the last one.

Top with handfuls of spinach and fill the slow cooker with it.

If you can't get them all together, let the first batch cook first and add a little more spinach.

Cook for 3 or 4 hours on medium heat until the turnips are soft.

Scrape the sides and serve.

Carrots and onions with Thai watercress

INGREDIENTS

1 ½ pounds carrots, peeled and cut into 1-inch pieces

½ onion, thinly sliced

cup of water

½ vegetable stock cube, crushed

1 tablespoon. extra virgin olive oil

1 tablespoon. sesame oil

½ teaspoon Thai chili paste

½ teaspoon Sriracha hot sauce

½ teaspoon chili powder

2 Thai bird's eye chilies, minced

Black pepper

½ pound watercress, thinly sliced

Put all the ingredients in a slow cooker, except the last one.

Garnish with a few handfuls of watercress and fill the slow cooker with it.

If you can't get them all together, let the first batch cook first and add a little more watercress.

Cook for 3 or 4 hours over medium heat until the carrots are tender.

Scrape the sides and serve.

baked pastry and sweet potatoes

INGREDIENTS

½ pound purslane, peeled and cut into 1-inch pieces

1 pound sweet potatoes, peeled and cut into 1-inch pieces

½ onion, thinly sliced

cup of water

½ vegetable stock cube, crushed

1 tablespoon. extra virgin olive oil

Black pepper

½ pound fresh spinach, coarsely chopped

Put all the ingredients in a slow cooker, except the last one.

Top with handfuls of spinach and fill the slow cooker with it.

If you can't get them all together, let the first batch cook first and add a little more spinach.

Cook for 3 or 4 hours on medium heat until the potatoes are tender.

Scrape the sides and serve.

White yam and baked potatoes

INGREDIENTS

½ pound potatoes, peeled and cut into 1-inch pieces

½ pound white pudding, peeled and cut into 1-inch pieces

½ pound carrots, peeled and cut into 1-inch pieces

½ red onion, thinly sliced

cup of water

½ vegetable stock cube, crushed

1 tablespoon. extra virgin olive oil

½ teaspoon cumin

½ teaspoon ground coriander

½ teaspoon garam masala

½ teaspoon cayenne pepper

Black pepper

½ pound fresh spinach, coarsely chopped

Put all the ingredients in a slow cooker, except the last one.

Top with handfuls of spinach and fill the slow cooker with it.

If you can't get them all together, let the first batch cook first and add a little more spinach.

Cook for 3 or 4 hours on medium heat until the potatoes are tender.

Scrape the sides and serve.

Hungarian parsnips and turnips

INGREDIENTS

½ pound turnips, peeled and cut into 1-inch pieces

½ pound carrots, peeled and cut into 1-inch pieces

½ pound parsley, peeled and cut into 1-inch pieces

½ red onion, thinly sliced

cup of water

½ vegetable stock cube, crushed

1 tablespoon. extra virgin olive oil

½ teaspoon paprika powder

½ tsp. chili powder

Black pepper

½ pound fresh spinach, coarsely chopped

Put all the ingredients in a slow cooker, except the last one.

Top with handfuls of spinach and fill the slow cooker with it.

If you can't get them all together, let the first batch cook first and add a little more spinach.

Cook for 3 or 4 hours on medium heat until the turnips are soft.

Scrape the sides and serve.

Plain Roasted Spinach

INGREDIENTS

1 ½ pounds broccoli, peeled and cut into 1-inch pieces

½ red onion, thinly sliced

cup of vegetable soup

1 tablespoon. extra virgin olive oil

½ teaspoon Italian seasoning

½ teaspoon chili powder

Black pepper

½ pound fresh spinach, coarsely chopped

Put all the ingredients in a slow cooker, except the last one.

Top with handfuls of spinach and fill the slow cooker with it.

If you can't get them all together, let the first batch cook first and add a little more spinach.

Cook for 3 or 4 hours over medium heat until the broccoli is tender.

Scrape the sides and serve.

Roasted Southeast Asian Spinach and Carrots

INGREDIENTS

½ pound turnips, peeled and cut into 1-inch pieces

½ pound carrots, peeled and cut into 1-inch pieces

½ pound parsley, peeled and cut into 1-inch pieces

½ red onion, thinly sliced

½ cup vegetable broth

1 tablespoon. extra virgin olive oil

½ teaspoon grated ginger

2 lemon stalks

8 cloves of garlic, minced

Black pepper

½ pound fresh spinach, coarsely chopped

Put all the ingredients in a slow cooker, except the last one.

Top with handfuls of spinach and fill the slow cooker with it.

If you can't get them all together, let the first batch cook first and add a little more spinach.

Cook for 3 or 4 hours on medium heat until the turnips are soft.

Scrape the sides and serve.

Roasted Kale and Brussels Sprouts

INGREDIENTS

1 ½ pounds Brussels sprouts, peeled and cut into 1-inch pieces

½ red onion, thinly sliced

cup of water

½ vegetable stock cube, crushed

1 tablespoon. extra virgin olive oil

½ teaspoon chili powder

Black pepper

½ pound kale, thinly sliced

Put all the ingredients in a slow cooker, except the last one.

Top with handfuls of kale and fill the slow cooker with it.

If you can't get them all together, let the first batch cook first and add a little more kale.

Cook for 3 hours on medium heat until the Brussels sprouts are tender.

Scrape the sides and serve.

Spinach and baked potatoes

INGREDIENTS

1 ½ pounds potatoes, peeled and cut into 1-inch pieces

½ onion, thinly sliced

cup of water

½ vegetable stock cube, crushed

1 tablespoon. extra virgin olive oil

½ teaspoon cumin

½ teaspoon ground coriander

½ teaspoon garam masala

½ teaspoon chili powder

Black pepper

½ pound fresh spinach, coarsely chopped

Put all the ingredients in a slow cooker, except the last one.

Top with handfuls of spinach and fill the slow cooker with it.

If you can't get them all together, let the first batch cook first and add a little more spinach.

Cook for 3 or 4 hours on medium heat until the potatoes are tender.

Scrape the sides and serve.

Sweet potatoes with curry and kale

INGREDIENTS

1 ½ pounds sweet potatoes, peeled and cut into 1-inch pieces

½ onion, thinly sliced

cup of water

½ vegetable stock cube, crushed

1 tablespoon. extra virgin olive oil

½ teaspoon cumin

½ teaspoon ground coriander

½ teaspoon garam masala

½ teaspoon chili powder

Black pepper

½ pound kale, thinly sliced

Put all the ingredients in a slow cooker, except the last one.

Top with handfuls of kale and fill the slow cooker with it.

If you can't get them all together, let the first batch cook first and add a little more kale.

Cook for 3 or 4 hours over medium heat until the sweet potatoes are tender.

Scrape the sides and serve.

Jalapeno Watercress and Parsnip

INGREDIENTS

1 ½ pounds parsley, peeled and cut into 1-inch pieces

½ red onion, thinly sliced

cup of water

½ vegetable stock cube, crushed

1 tablespoon. extra virgin olive oil

½ teaspoon cumin

½ teaspoon jalapeño pepper, minced

1 ancho pepper, minced

Black pepper

½ pound watercress, thinly sliced

Put all the ingredients in a slow cooker, except the last one.

Top with handfuls of spinach and fill the slow cooker with it.

If you can't get them all together, let the first batch cook first and add a little more spinach.

Cook for 3 or 4 hours over medium heat until the parsley is tender.

Scrape the sides and serve.

Watercress and broccoli in chili garlic sauce

INGREDIENTS

1 ½ pounds carrots, peeled and cut into 1-inch pieces

½ pound broccoli, peeled and cut into 1-inch pieces

½ onion, thinly sliced

cup of water

½ vegetable stock cube, crushed

1 tablespoon. sesame oil

½ teaspoon chili garlic sauce

½ tsp. lime juice

½ tsp. chopped green onions

Black pepper

½ pound watercress, thinly sliced

Put all the ingredients in a slow cooker, except the last one.

Garnish with a few handfuls of watercress and fill the slow cooker with it.

If you can't get them all together, let the first batch cook first and add a little more watercress.

Cook for 3 or 4 hours over medium heat until the carrots are tender.

Scrape the sides and serve.

Spicy Bok Choy and Broccoli

INGREDIENTS

1 pound broccoli, peeled and cut into 1-inch pieces

½ pound button mushrooms, sliced

½ onion, thinly sliced

cup of water

½ vegetable stock cube, crushed

1 tablespoon. sesame oil

½ teaspoon Chinese five spice powder

½ teaspoon Sichuan pepper

½ teaspoon chili powder

Black pepper

½ pound bok choy, thinly sliced

Put all the ingredients in a slow cooker, except the last one.

Make handfuls of bok choy and fill the slow cooker with it.

If you can't fit them all together, let the first batch cook first and add a little more bok choy.

Cook for 3 or 4 hours over medium heat until the broccoli is tender.

Scrape the sides and serve.

Spinach and shiitake mushrooms

INGREDIENTS

1 ½ pounds cauliflower, peeled and cut into 1-inch pieces

½ pound shiitake mushrooms, sliced

½ red onion, thinly sliced

cup of vegetable soup

2 tablespoons. sesame seed oil

½ teaspoon of vinegar

½ teaspoon garlic, minced

Black pepper

½ pound fresh spinach, coarsely chopped

Put all the ingredients in a slow cooker, except the last one.

Top with handfuls of spinach and fill the slow cooker with it.

If you can't get them all together, let the first batch cook first and add a little more spinach.

Cook for 3 or 4 hours over medium heat until the cauliflower is tender.

Scrape the sides and serve.

Spinach and potatoes with pesto

INGREDIENTS

1 ½ pounds potatoes, peeled and cut into 1-inch pieces

½ onion, thinly sliced

cup of vegetable soup

1 tablespoon. extra virgin olive oil

2 tablespoons. pesto sauce

Black pepper

½ pound fresh spinach, coarsely chopped

Put all the ingredients in a slow cooker, except the last one.

Top with handfuls of spinach and fill the slow cooker with it.

If you can't get them all together, let the first batch cook first and add a little more spinach.

Cook for 3 or 4 hours on medium heat until the potatoes are tender.

Scrape the sides and serve.

Roasted Sweet Potatoes and Kale

INGREDIENTS

1 ½ pounds sweet potatoes, peeled and cut into 1-inch pieces

½ onion, thinly sliced

cup of vegetable soup

1 tablespoon. extra virgin olive oil

2 tablespoons. red curry powder

Black pepper

½ pound fresh kale, thinly sliced

Put all the ingredients in a slow cooker, except the last one.

Top with handfuls of kale and fill the slow cooker with it.

If you can't fit them all together, let the first batch cook first and add a little more greens.

Cook for 3 or 4 hours over medium heat until the sweet potatoes are tender.

Scrape the sides and serve.

Turnip greens and turnips with pesto sauce

INGREDIENTS

1 ½ pounds turnips, peeled and cut into 1-inch pieces

½ onion, thinly sliced

cup of vegetable soup

1 tablespoon. extra virgin olive oil

2 tablespoons. pesto sauce

Black pepper

½ pound fresh turnip greens, coarsely chopped

Put all the ingredients in a slow cooker, except the last one.

Top with a few handfuls of turnip greens and fill the slow cooker with them.

If you can't fit them all together, let the first batch cook first and add a few more turnip greens.

Cook for 3 or 4 hours on medium heat until the turnips are soft.

Scrape the sides and serve.

Swiss chard and carrots with pesto

INGREDIENTS

1 ½ pounds carrots, peeled and cut into 1-inch pieces

½ red onion, thinly sliced

cup of vegetable soup

2 tablespoons. extra virgin olive oil

3 tablespoons. pesto sauce

Black pepper

½ pound fresh Swiss chard, coarsely chopped

Put all the ingredients in a slow cooker, except the last one.

Top with handfuls of Swiss chard and fill the slow cooker with it.

If you can't put them all together at once, cook the first batch first and add a little more Swiss chard.

Cook for 3 or 4 hours over medium heat until the carrots are tender.

Scrape the sides and serve.

Bok Choy and Carrots in a Chili Garlic Sauce

INGREDIENTS

1 ½ pounds carrots, peeled and cut into 1-inch pieces

½ onion, thinly sliced

cup of vegetable soup

1 tablespoon. sesame oil

4 cloves of garlic, minced

2 tablespoons. chili garlic sauce

Black pepper

½ pound fresh Bok Choy, thinly sliced

Put all the ingredients in a slow cooker, except the last one.

Make handfuls of Bok Choy and fill the slow cooker with it.

If you can't get them all together, let the first batch cook first and add a little more Bok Choy.

Cook for 3 or 4 hours over medium heat until the carrots are tender.

Scrape the sides and serve.

Slow Cooked Turnip Greens and Parsley

INGREDIENTS

1 ½ pounds parsley, peeled and cut into 1-inch pieces

½ onion, thinly sliced

cup of vegetable soup

1 tablespoon. extra virgin olive oil

Black pepper

½ pound fresh turnip greens, coarsely chopped

Put all the ingredients in a slow cooker, except the last one.

Top with handfuls of spinach and fill the slow cooker with it.

If you can't get them all together, let the first batch cook first and add a little more spinach.

Cook for 3 or 4 hours on medium heat until the potatoes are tender.

Scrape the sides and serve.

Slow Cooked Kale and Broccoli

INGREDIENTS

1 ½ pounds broccoli florets

½ onion, thinly sliced

cup of vegetable soup

1 tablespoon. extra virgin olive oil

2 tablespoons. pesto sauce

Black pepper

½ pound fresh kale, thinly sliced

Put all the ingredients in a slow cooker, except the last one.

Top with handfuls of kale and fill the slow cooker with it.

If you can't get them all together, let the first batch cook first and add a little more kale.

Cook for 3 to 4 hours over medium heat until the broccoli florets are tender.

Scrape the sides and serve.

Endive and carrots stewed in pesto

INGREDIENTS

1 ½ pounds carrots, peeled and cut into 1-inch pieces

½ onion, thinly sliced

cup of vegetable soup

1 tablespoon. extra virgin olive oil

2 tablespoons. pesto sauce

Black pepper

½ pound fresh endives, coarsely chopped

Put all the ingredients in a slow cooker, except the last one.

Garnish with a few handfuls of fennel and fill the slow cooker with them.

If you can't get them all together, let the first batch cook first and add a little more endive.

Cook for 3 or 4 hours over medium heat until the carrots are tender.

Scrape the sides and serve.

Braised Romaine Lettuce and Brussels Sprouts

INGREDIENTS

1 ½ pounds Brussels sprouts

½ onion, thinly sliced

cup of vegetable soup

1 tablespoon. extra virgin olive oil

Black pepper

½ pound fresh romaine lettuce, thinly sliced

Put all the ingredients in a slow cooker, except the last one.

Top with handfuls of lettuce and fill the slow cooker with it.

If you can't get them all together, let the first batch cook first and add a little more romaine lettuce.

Cook for 3 hours on medium heat until the Brussels sprouts are tender.

Scrape the sides and serve.

Endive and boiled potatoes

INGREDIENTS

1 ½ pounds potatoes, peeled and cut into 1-inch pieces

½ onion, thinly sliced

cup of vegetable soup

1 tablespoon. extra virgin olive oil

1 C. Italian seasoning

Black pepper

½ pound fresh endives, coarsely chopped

Put all the ingredients in a slow cooker, except the last one.

Top with handfuls of spinach and fill the slow cooker with it.

If you can't get them all together, let the first batch cook first and add a little more spinach.

Cook for 3 or 4 hours on medium heat until the potatoes are tender.

Scrape the sides and serve.

Turnip greens and turnips slow cooked in vegan butter

INGREDIENTS

1 ½ pounds turnips, peeled and cut into 1-inch pieces

½ onion, thinly sliced

cup of vegetable soup

4 tablespoons. vegan butter or margarine

2 tablespoons. lime juice

3 cloves of garlic, minced

Black pepper

½ pound fresh turnip greens, coarsely chopped

Put all the ingredients in a slow cooker, except the last one.

Top with a few handfuls of turnip greens and fill the slow cooker with them.

If you can't fit them all together, let the first batch cook first and add a few more turnip greens.

Cook for 3 or 4 hours on medium heat until the turnips are soft.

Scrape the sides and serve.

Kale and Parsnip Slow Cooked in Vegan Butter

INGREDIENTS

1 ½ pounds parsley, peeled and cut into 1-inch pieces

½ onion, thinly sliced

cup of vegetable soup

4 tablespoons. melted vegan butter

2 tablespoons. lemon juice

Black pepper

½ pound fresh kale, thinly sliced

Put all the ingredients in a slow cooker, except the last one.

Top with handfuls of kale and fill the slow cooker with it.

If you can't get them all together, let the first batch cook first and add a little more kale.

Cook for 3 or 4 hours over medium heat until the parsley is tender.

Scrape the sides and serve.

Chinese Style Spinach and Carrots

INGREDIENTS

1 ½ pounds carrots, peeled and cut into 1-inch pieces

½ onion, thinly sliced

cup of vegetable soup

1 tablespoon. sesame oil

2 tablespoons. hoisin sauce

Black pepper

½ pound fresh spinach, coarsely chopped

Put all the ingredients in a slow cooker, except the last one.

Top with handfuls of spinach and fill the slow cooker with it.

If you can't get them all together, let the first batch cook first and add a little more spinach.

Cook for 3 or 4 hours over medium heat until the carrots are tender.

Scrape the sides and serve.

Bok Choy and Stewed Carrots

INGREDIENTS

1 ½ pounds carrots, peeled and cut into 1-inch pieces

½ onion, thinly sliced

cup of vegetable soup

1 tablespoon. sesame oil

1 tablespoon. canola oil

2 tablespoons. hoisin sauce

Black pepper

½ pound fresh Bok Choy, thinly sliced

Put all the ingredients in a slow cooker, except the last one.

Make handfuls of bok choy and fill the slow cooker with it.

If you can't fit them all together, let the first batch cook first and add a little more bok choy.

Cook for 3 or 4 hours over medium heat until the carrots are tender.

Scrape the sides and serve.

Micro greens and slow cooked potatoes

INGREDIENTS

1 ½ pounds potatoes, peeled and cut into 1-inch pieces

½ onion, thinly sliced

cup of vegetable soup

2 tablespoons. extra virgin olive oil

1 C. annatto seeds

1 C. cumin

1 C. lime juice

Black pepper

½ pound fresh greens, coarsely chopped

Put all the ingredients in a slow cooker, except the last one.

Add handfuls of micro greens and fill the slow cooker with them.

If you can't fit them all together, let the first batch cook first and add some micro greens.

Cook for 3 or 4 hours on medium heat until the potatoes are tender.

Scrape the sides and serve.

Kale leaves and slow cooked potatoes

INGREDIENTS

1 ½ pounds sweet potatoes, peeled and cut into 1-inch pieces

½ onion, thinly sliced

cup of vegetable soup

1 tablespoon. extra virgin olive oil

2 tablespoons. pesto sauce

Black pepper

½ pound fresh kale, thinly sliced

Put all the ingredients in a slow cooker, except the last one.

Top with handfuls of kale and fill the slow cooker with it.

If you can't fit them all together, let the first batch cook first and add a little more greens.

Cook for 3 or 4 hours over medium heat until the sweet potatoes are tender.

Scrape the sides and serve.

Slow Cooker Cabbage and Potatoes

INGREDIENTS

1 ½ pounds potatoes, peeled and cut into 1-inch pieces

½ onion, thinly sliced

cup of vegetable soup

1 tablespoon. extra virgin olive oil

Black pepper

½ pound fresh purple cabbage, thinly sliced

Put all the ingredients in a slow cooker, except the last one.

Top with handfuls of purple cabbage and fill the slow cooker with it.

If you can't fit them all in at once, cook the first batch first and add a little more kale.

Cook for 3 or 4 hours on medium heat until the potatoes are tender.

Scrape the sides and serve.

Boiled cabbage and carrots

INGREDIENTS

1 ½ pounds carrots, peeled and cut into 1-inch pieces

½ onion, thinly sliced

cup of vegetable soup

1 tablespoon. extra virgin olive oil

Black pepper

½ pound fresh cabbage, thinly sliced

Put all the ingredients in a slow cooker, except the last one.

Top with handfuls of cabbage and fill the slow cooker with it.

If you can't get them all together, let the first batch cook first and add a little more cabbage.

Cook for 3 or 4 hours over medium heat until the carrots are tender.

Scrape the sides and serve.

www.ingramcontent.com/pod-product-compliance
Lightning Source LLC
Chambersburg PA
CBHW071856110526
44591CB00011B/1440